Can I make everybody happy?

Collected writings by*
Dag Brandsaeter
& Noa Segal

**This book express the email-exhange between clients and designers on ten different projects. All names mentioned are fictional.*

This book was made possible thanks to (best kept anonymous) beloved friends and colleagues!

About an art book

Thank you for the second proposal.

It's hard to say this, but the design is again so far from what we had in mind that we don't think the collaboration will be possible. It is very important to us to not have a concept on top of the project.

We're trying to challenge the readers to see this work as 'real art' – like museum art – even though it is made by non-artists. So we think a more traditional (but great looking) art book is still radical in this context. We don't want to re-imagine the concept of the Art Book – because that will work against the attempt to re-imagine the concepts of Art and the Artist. We need the book to be somewhat straight-forward, so we can work against that, use it to bring authority to the work.

We apologise for not fully understanding how conceptual your work is at the beginning; I think we only saw the look of the samples and not always the ideas behind them. Or perhaps we can appreciate the concepts better when they are applied to other people's art. In any case, we are disappointed that this could not work out, and will continue to admire your work from afar.

Best,

About a book cover

Hi,

I like both the colors. Generally, I think blue-green is the most beautiful color there is, but lilac feels more spiritual, has more substance and will probably fit this more, even though the blue-green is more beautiful. The text on the back as a headline should create an initial feeling, without explaining it all. That should be first. Could also be placed on top of the page. Then a space, followed by the explanation text and the regular information.

The script font on the back I don't like at all, it's too hard and square. Doesn't fit the concept. It needs to be more careful looking. It is important to get away from the seventies feeling. It doesn't fit the concept. It should be something that contrasts with the logo. Attached are a few examples from Cinderella again. It doesn't have to look exactly like it, but the softness in there is important to communicate. It has noclear answers, it asks questions. Maybe it is like this, maybe not. It's the sensibility that needs to be communicated, just like it is done on the first page, where not the aesthetics of the font– but the image is the thing. You should not understand it all, but start wondering.

See you tomorrow,

About a magazine

Hello,

We are sending you the material we have collected so far tomorrow, for you to start thinking and designing the magazine. As soon as we have all the images and translations together with little details like titles, biographies etc. we will let you know by e-mail and send them with DHL. We have been discussing the issue concerning the overall appearance of the magazine and we have some suggestions for you to consider:

Cover (front and back), we would like a spine binding instead of staples. We are a bit concerned about the cover being only text, perhaps just image and text on the back? Or any other ideas? For the paper, we are quite concerned about the quality of the stock. The only trouble is that the images in the magazine you showed look a bit pale and thus lose their visual strength. Is it possible to use a good quality paper similar to Bidoun's standards?

Just to summarise: because the magazine now works as a space for the artists to create specific projects, it should have a long shelf life, and the design should follow this idea. We feel that the design should act as a project in itself, thus offering a new dimension.

Looking forward,

About an Identity

Dear,

After the presentation of your design I spoke to the board members. Unfortunately Johanna was away for a few days, so these comments come a few days later. I have to be honest with you: the board members were not too happy with the design. Maybe it was not entirely clear to you what we are looking for. We want to give you the opportunity to finish this work, but in view of the opinion of the board I think you will have to present something completely different. That is to say, to start all over again.

Underneath I'll try to summarise the comments of the board members on the design you presented.

The organisation wants to improve its image and wants to be fresh and cheerful, light and full of expectations. The design you presented is just the opposite. The logo, the material, the colours and the font make everything serious and heavy. Some board members said it was too sixties, too old fashioned. Some said it was too North-European and it should be more Mediterranian (I hope you understand what they mean with this, they try to point out an atmosphere). It should be light and elegant instead of heavy and a little stiff. The visiting card is, in the opinion of some members, only nice if you see it in the context of the whole design. If you see it without the other things you miss the design, it's too much like a small piece of cardboard. And then there are some practical things: the brochure should be more like a flyer, light and not heavy in weight, because we don't want to use too many stamps. The font you used for the letters will require a lot of ink, and it's very hard to work with it on the computer screen.

I'm sorry about all this, but I think it's better to tell you everything frankly, so it can help you to give it another try, that's to say, if you are willing to give it another try. It can just have been a misinterpretation of the assignment. I want to ask you if you want to make another design. The only thing is, there is not much time left. Will you be able to present something within a week?

I do hope that you understand that a new housestyle is very important to us and we all have to be happy with it. This will count for the second design as well. We can't go through with it if we're not happy with it.

If you have questions or want to talk about all this, you can contact me anytime.

With kind regards,

About a layout

COVER
1– The barcode should be moved further down, parallel with the "£6.95."

2– The logo should be moved down to the middle of the white margin on the book spine.

PAGE NUMBERS
I reached an agreement with the designer before I left. The page numbers should be counted from the very first page of the book. It would make up 56 pages instead of the present 50. Page numbers should appear on the bottom left and right corners of the page.

HEADINGS
Each heading of a poem should be aligned with the left beginning of the main body of the text. This change will be very important.

There are three dedication poems. The heading and the dedication should not be jumbled together.

For Stephen Spender

At Hawthornden Castle

For Pamela Egremont
This poem

For Warwick Gould

About my bio, line 10 "(handprinted in 1983 and circulated privately and secretly)", please put "in the year of 1983".

As for the last two lines of A day within days, "My China, My China", I left them out as Peter and I went over the text several times. He said, "If I were you, I would leave them out". I took his suggestion, but if you think it is important to put them back in, please do, as you are the editor of my book. I wish I had more of these chances to honour my editor.

Is it possible to make the barcode smaller?

Please also reposition the body of text of the following poems on the page. Generally speaking, they should all be moved down a bit.

Boyhood (3) image (6) red wine (7) an autumn leaf & Football (8) within the colour of night (9) waiting (11) voice (19) To. c.J. (24,25) In the bathroom (27) learning a new Language (28) chance & discovery (30) desire hotel (32) A prayer & i see (33) the unfamiliar customs house (34,35) Listening to chinese music (44) only one way (45) insomnia (46) Standing at the doors of dusk (47) At Hawthornden Castle (48) this poem (49).

Some changes regarding the headings, page numbering etc. Both the designer and Michael have agreed to react on our mutual agreement. It is a pity that nothing has been done. It is mainly Michael's personal preference. I would like to urge him to abide by the convention and tradition.

I still have the right to declare that I have nothing to do with this book. I am certainly not proud of being part of your tradtion or convention, let me put it straight.

I hope you have had a good time in Italy. I think I should thank you for your labour on the book, if it still looks like my book.

With my very best wishes,

About a catalogue

Hello,

I finally got the time to write to you after having received your proposal for the catalogue. During these 24 hours I was madly involved with exhausting telephone calls from Israel and Germany. As for the cover, I saw it only a few hours ago!! As you know we stopped everything for now in order to make the English corrections. The point is that one of the most famous historians of design reviewed the text and found it stylistically unacceptable. So we do not want to run the risk of publishing something that is not really good. I would like to use this break time opportunity to make some changes to the graphical layout.

1- I did not yet have the opportunity to interact with you as I got the first and final proposal only yesterday night from the other curator. He is more important than me as he is an academic and would not like to sign something he did not see. He had not had the opportunity to see the catalogue at all. He selected the works that will appear there and signs the text. We should be given more time for supervision. I believe that a real work between a graphic designer and a curator should be built through interaction and finally the customer should receive a product that he finds good. I thank you for the amount of work that you have been through, and I know you had a hard, stressful time, both physically and psychologically. I liked the invitation and the layout for the objects in the catalogue very much. I think the shopping trolley was a successful choice which we will repeat in other graphic layouts like: the 16m long sign in front of the exhibition, entrance signs inside the building in front of our exhibition, 70 x 100cm posters, etc. At this point I do not see why it should not also be used for the front cover of the catalogue!

2– The sentence “Is there such an animal?” should go on the back cover (4th page of the cover), not on the front cover. This sentence hides the names of some of the designers: yellow disappears on white and the black attracts too much unnecessary attention. The sponsors in Israel also do not want this sentence to be too aggressive and visible. Another reason to put the sentence on the back links to the fact that Hebrew books are 'upside-down', so the back is the front. I think, that another possible solution is to at least make the designers names emerge out of the black, so that when the black overlaps the name of a designer, the black print is opened (cut) to let out the yellow, orange or possibly more evident colours that might be chosen. I know you wanted the names only as a background but it is not fair that some names are legible and others are not. Some of the names of the above, mentioned designers are also spelled incorrectly. I will send you the corrections separately.

3– And now the animals, the hardest subject …
I agree with you that we do not want just a traditional,

boring catalogue, but there are many ways to be noticed and not all of them are good. I don't feel comfortable looking at the animal images and they do not integrate with the rest. For instance, I do not want to have them next to my text. Lastly, this catalogue is a very important event for Israeli design, and I cannot afford to make mistakes. I am the curator and therefor responsible for the image we will give, so please, I ask you to remove all the animals and to look for some other solution to fill the space or to leave it as open space: better nothing than something unpleasant. I showed it to a few people to get feedback and did not find one that liked it, neither were they curious to know what it meant. I am checking if it is possible to get the copyright for some images from a cartoonist who created a duck which is the typical Israeli Donald Duck and ironically depicts Israeli life. Maybe we could take it as the animal. I hope you understand my point.

I have a big responsibility and am also under incredible time pressure for many works involved in the exhibition. I hope you will be able to understand our points and find a compromise to meet our requirements.

Best regards and Happy Easter,

Hello,

I appreciate you trying to make changes to the project. Finally we start having the usual kind of relationship between a client and a graphic designer. I am sorry to know that you decided to resign before the work is finished. However, I accept your resignation. I don't know what kind of relationship you usually have with your clients, but I doubt you present the final work as a fact that the client should accept without any opportunity to make changes, as you did in our case. I had no sketch or even two different proposals all along the process. I got the cover two hours before you planned to go to print. I think that even Michelangelo did not have this kind of luxury. I understand the amount of work you did under constantly changing conditions, but it is not a good enough excuse for why I couldn't see sketches of your ideas in advance to discuss.

I sent the catalogue PDF to Prof. F. (that he never got from you) without telling him anything. I was curious to hear his opinion. When I asked him what he thought about the catalogue he mentioned certain designs that we chose and that he liked the layout etc. Finally I asked him, what do you think about the animals? He told me ... but these are dummy images, why do you ask? Later he told me that next time we will do the catalogue in Italy.

I am afraid I will not have a next time. Making the first important international exhibition of Israeli design it is unacceptable to print the catalogue with black and white animal images that have nothing to do with the text or with Israel. We speak in the text about Israeli humour. Well, people will say they don't understand our humour. I find it offensive when you tell me that you want to do 'a product of high quality', as if we (the unsophisticated people) want to do a product of low quality. I don't have any disagreement with you about doing an 'original' catalogue, but I disagree with your artistic choice. An American teenager who undergoes tongue spliting plastic surgery wants to be original. I don't find it so. All the people that see the invitation make you compliment about the choice of unusual art work that has the Israeli humour. So we want, in a reasonable way, to have the same trolley also on the cover. We are not convinced with the concept of "Is there such an animal?" Prof.F. would like to cancel it. I say "we could live with it". It is not clear to Israelis, not speaking about others. Maybe it is necessary to add a small * with a literal and figurative translation. This page might be inside the back cover, which is coherent with a Hebrew font, or as an internal cover where you put the animals. We are not enthusiastic about the fifties B movies but it is as far as we can go to sustain your concept. The title "Is there such an animal?" can appear for the second time between the science fiction images to make the concept clearer. Of course it is possible to take out the animals and leave empty pages. It is better to have 'purely beautiful' or 'pleasant' for 'everyone' than an embarrassing document.

I wish you a Happy Easter,

About a cover

Hello,

Just getting back to you on the material we have received to date from the designer. For the record, my conversation with the designers on this was a bit bizarre. We have received one cover idea to date, following on from the meeting we had here in our offices with Maria and the designers several weeks ago. We have reviewed this cover idea with two of our sales and marketing people and one of our in-house designers with the following comments, which Maria asked that we provide the designers with. I am copying this to you first so that we might avoid further confusion on this project. As you have appointed the designers, I think it appropriate that you deal with them on this.

The price and barcode information, our logo, your logo and our recycled logo are all to go on the back cover. This all takes up a substantial amount of space, so we don't believe the treatment of the price on the current front cover is feasible. If the designer wishes to use the barcode as a 'commercial' device on the front cover, fine, as long as this works with the rest of the front cover design. We are sending the designer our guidelines on how to use our identity on the book's front cover, spine and back cover. Generally, the current cover design doesn't provide a clear idea of what the book is about. We have asked for several other alternatives, hence these notes. Normally our designers would do up about ten to twenty different cover ideas for us to discuss further with marketing and sales.

The use of the contributor names on the front cover we like, but we think more benefit could be gained from the associations that might be made with the better known contributors.

The image used on the front cover at the moment is too small. We think the cover could really benefit either from the use of an image or images (i.e. being used to greater effect) or being treated as a typographic exercise in its own right.

We think there should be a general sub-title to accompany the book's title, as this isn't clear to anyone not familiar with the project. Perhaps you can come up with something more accessible as a sub-title.

As for the designers notes on the paper he would like to use, we are happy to work along these lines and will identify a paper as best we can that is a match, given what they want within the budget we are working with.
The printing of the book will be in Pantone 6U black, as per our agreement with you.

Again, I think it might help for you to correspond with the designer, as we seem to have started on a bum note. Our interest is to develope a title that is as commercial as possible given the material we are working with. A strong cover will help sell the book in the general trade. As for the specialist trade, we are less concerned about this as it more or less looks after itself without us having to do much about it. In other words, it would be helpful if the designer were to work with us in developing a strong cover for the conventional book trade along the lines of what we have experienced in selling to that sector. If we can't do this, we will be left with the specialist art/design book and museum trade, which doesn't warrant printing more than 1,000 to 1,500 copies. This isn't what we signed up for with you, and it certainly isn't enough for us to recoup our own investment in this project.

If you'd like any further clarification regarding anything I have set out above, just let me know. Otherwise, I look forward to receiving the rest of the book's content from you so that we can start editing it to then send on to the designer for setting.

Best,

Hello,

I received the comments from the publisher yesterday regarding your first layout of the book and the cover. What is your reaction to this?

Our comments are that what you have presented so far looks really good, but we agree that it might be good to present some alternative covers. Not as many as 20 though. We also like the idea of putting the contributors names on the cover, and if you can come up with additional ideas on how to present them it would be great.

The publisher seems concerned that the cover doesn't communicate what the book is about and would like us to think of a sub-title. We will work on this and get back to you with a suggestion. Please get back to me with your thoughts on this as soon as possible. And one very important thing – can you invoice us your graphic design fee, as well as the cost of the info-sheets this fall? I would need to have both of these invoices within this week if possible.

Thanks so much!

Hi,

Thanks for these. We reviewed these covers at our meeting this morning, and we have the following feedback:

Generally, people didn't like cover 3 – the red and green together was too Christmas-y and the green box was reminiscent of Benetton. We really liked covers 2 and 4, and would like to see if there is a way of merging the two: perhaps the green background and image of cover 4 with the typeface of cover 2? We like the sub-title "On Contemporary Art and Collaborative Practices best, and it was felt that the sub-title should appear directly below, or closer to Taking the Matter ... than it does in either of these two cover options, and that the title and sub-title should be closer in point size than they already are.

Regarding the back cover, the barcode and price will have to go on the back, as there will be more than one price and barcode, so this information would take up too much space on the front cover. The names of the contributors could go either on the front or back cover – perhaps we could try a few options and see what looks best. There will also be back cover text, which either the client can supply or we can do something up here for the client to check.

OK, that's all for now, I hope that's helpful.

Best,

Hello,

I must say that I like all covers.

It would be good to consider back and front together to be able to discuss further. Or how do you think of these things at the publisher? I think it is useful with the names of the contributors on the front.

Best,

About an artist book

Dear,

This is the first I hear about your approach to the cover at the end of the project. I can't work that way and need you to proceed as we have been doing thus far. I trust you understand why but I will mention a few reasons:

The cover sets the tone for the entire book. It's essential for David to have the jacket available for marketing purposes. The cover has already been through many passes and we have yet to agree on a direction. The cover has specific expense implications that I must know in advance. It would be irresponsible of me to leave this for the end especially considering the conflicting opinions about how to proceed.

Please send me revised layouts.

Indeed I am eager to proceed with the content but reiterate that you have what you need to do sample revised layouts of the book, including text and illustrations.

Thank you,

Dear ,

I tried to reach you by phone this morning while you were in a meeting. Apparently I will be in a meeting when you are available so I am using e-mail as an interim means of communication until we talk.

First I want to again express my regret about yesterday. No matter what the circumstances, there is simply no need for you to be the recipient of rude behavior. I regret you were put in this position.

I am hopeful we can work together to achieve the shared goal of having the best possible book in time for the opening. We have a different approach to layout of photographs, but I am eager to understand your approach and ask that we meet each other half way on this point. To that end I would like to make the following comments:

1. After review of my essay layout, I want to cut photos that I think are too folkloric and really don't complement the text. Under separate cover I am sending the essay with notations of what should be cut and the relevant changes to the figure references. I have a clearer understanding of some of the cropping questions I had before, others I would still like to talk about.

2. I see that you have changed the number font but this has deleted all the fractions in the dimensions, and the font you had is clearly better in relation to the other typeface so it is preferable to go back to what you had before. If I had known this would be the case I would

have agreed to leave it as is. Now I realize the contrast with the current font is really awkward.

3. We have a copyright problem with the photo on the catalogue entry opener. Unfortunately that image will have to be replaced. The same for the photo in my introduction. I know this comes late in the game.
I would like to replace the photo in my introduction and then move the editor's note under the title to the right hand page and simply have no image there.

Please let me know if we can talk soon.

Thank you!

Dear,

I spoke to John a number of times, once you were on the phone and the other time in a meeting. I sent you three mails about the jacket. In any case, I have the printer's contact information and will send him the disks today. Today I am sending you the final version of the introduction. Stuart has the final pass of the manuscript. I expect it back no later than Monday. Peter will have to add information that is still missing. I prefer to send you the manuscript in its final form. You can definitely revise the layouts for the first section with the essay text you have had for a while. The changes relate to the illustrations. It's important that we have a better understanding of how you expect to handle the illustrations. The only version we have seen, we agreed needed to be revised. I would really like to see preliminary layouts for this essay. You also have a working disk of illustrations for the second section.

I am concerned about the cover. Based on the last layouts you sent it's clear that we do not have the same vision of how this should look. I am asking you to prepare other options based on the information I sent in my previous e-mails. Please try a cover option using cat. no. 1 and also one of the "white" pieces wrapping around the binding. I refer to this in my previous e-mail.

Thank you.

Dear,

We need to clarify some things so we can progress with appropriate input henceforth. Peter's comments have been and continue to be integral to this project, he can provide comments and contribute to the design in a way that I cannot.

I do not consider this punch-hitting in my absence. I am away and working. I am never absent from this project.

Thank you.

About a poster

Hey,

David is sick. Try to get to know how it's working with Johanna as fast as possible. Attached is the first set-up of text for the poster.

Best,

Hey,

I just got an image from the gallery; they would really like this image for the invitation/small poster and the A0 poster. The title hopefully comes today!

Greetings,

Hoi,

Below I have the mail Daniela sent me this morning about the title; 'Sinaasappelsap im Schiermoddergetriebe'. David wrote that he would like to have some influence on the layout and the typography of the invitation/poster, but first he wants to wait for your suggestions and then react on that.

Greets,

Hello,

I just got a mail from David saying he wants another title. It is kind of important that we show the invitation/poster (so, everything that goes out) to him first, as well as his assistant and the gallery owner.

Greetings,

Hi,

I just had Johanna on the phone (her fax is out of ink), and she has come up with a much more concise title for the show: (........) –Surrogat. The important thing is that the brackets are as long as the word 'surrogat', whereas the number of dots inside are less important. I know your deadline, but I hope it is still possible to change the title.

I am sorry :) Maybe you already arranged it with Frank, but if possible, I would ask you to send us the final layout before it goes to print.

Thank you!

Also a nice day to you,

Hey,

We managed to find a very good image from the film 'Skipholt', which Johanna would prefer to use. She will send you a fax with a sketch for the layout, and I will send you the slide. I will try to contact you later today and discuss some details. I am very sorry for the trouble, but I hope it will all work out fine!

Best wishes!

Hi,

Thanks for your answer; the problem is that the poster has to go to the printer next week Tuesday and our designer will not have enough time to make a completely new poster by then, so I'm afraid we will have to work with the proposals I sent you; I meant that there is still time to make some changes/corrections to the proposals I already sent; so please let me know which poster you like best and what should be changed if you have any suggestions.

I wish you great holidays!

Hi,

You will find a printable PDF from the designer's poster at http://www.xxxx.xx/xxx/xx_plakat_print.pdf.

There is also an 4C A3-large JPG of the scan at http://www.xxxx.xx/xxx/xx_plakat_print.jpg

It is a bit larger than 300 dpi - so there is enough picture for the bleed ...

Best,

Hey,

Do you know something about an ad in a German booklet/magazine ?

Best,

P.S. the poster turned out good!

About an Invitation

Hello,

Thank you for your very enthusiastic e-mail.

Unfortunately I have to say I am your worst nightmare. I am unable to involve myself in any collaborations at the moment since I am beyond busy in developing the artwork for the show itself. This has taken me over a year of planning and I now have 4 people working with me on this project, doing research and helping execute the drawings.

I am over-booked in May with my own work, site visits for other projects and people that are coming to visit me already, Anna included, to check on my work. So I am completely over-extended and quite stressed out already. Moreover, I am not a great fan of independent design, as I find it only creates obstacles for my work that I have to navigate around. It is a challenge I find completely irrelevant to my process, but a necessity to the PR. Whenever I hire designers for my own invites, posters and publications, which is very often, they always work directly under me and are given dead basic instructions. Otherwise, I find myself having to adapt my artwork to the parameters given, or the creative needs of the designers, and this creates only more work for me, such as now, finding a suitable image to crop for this stupid pre-determined invitation card for example. I hate this. I have already exchanged four e-mails with Johanna about it, when I could be drawing instead. Finally, I don't know if you are also designing the big map, but this is something I have become heavily involved with at the moment. It is very complex and will require both artistic and editorial overview on my part, co-ordinating both images and text with the final wall presentation - I simply don't want any other aesthetic to affect my own at this stage. I am not exactly sure if the poster you are referring to is also the map, or a separate item, but in either case, I will ask for and insist on classic SIMPLICITY in regards to type (Helvetica is my typeface), which hopefully is NOT placed on top of the images, but finds itself discreet and functional, giving maximum integrity possible to the artwork – my work. I look forward to your draft PDF of the invitation, and if you need a separate image for the poster, please send me the specs for it, and I will provide a high res when I have my work shot here in the studio on the 15th.

Greetings,

Hello Everybody!

Just for your information: I met Francesca and I have seen the drawings that she prepared for the exhibition. They are great! She finished already 20 of them, from which we could select one for the poster. The cd with all the photos should arrive here within the next days. As soon as I have them, we can make a selection together.

Greetings,

Hello,

Here's the image for the poster. The first version is in low resolution, for the sketch. The high resolution images I will send later on a cd.

Concerning the design: You can use the whole image and set a box above or below the image for the text, or you can cut the image and set the text in the middle of the image (for example in the black field). To make the whole thing a bit lively, we would like to have a coloured typeface, (that's also the wish of Francesca). Everything clear?

Thanks and greetings,

Hello,

Yeah, the selection was made together and Francesca is also informed and fine with it. If you want to have a look at the other images, here's the website ...

Greetings,

Hi,

Thanks for the suggestion. We had a look and we are not really happy with it. First of all, we think the collage out of two images is very confusing and the type is also not very readable. I think it would be better to work only with the image 'insula svissera' - probably also just with a cut-out or detail, so that the stroke of the marker, as proposed by you, is recognisable as such, and is peceived as marks at the border, which reference to a map. We would appreciate having the type overlaid in colour (maybe that contrasts even more) and, if it is possible, without interfering too much with the image and changing it.

The secondary information like exhibition date, opening hours and so on can be smaller. That's probably also what Francesca wishes to see. She always accentuates that she likes to have it very simple.

Thanks a lot and greetings,

Hi,

Thank you for this. I think the choice of the image, the font and the layout are very, very nice ... but with the overlay you can't really read it clearly or fast and as a poster, it should be an instant communication ... it doesn't really work. Also it took me a second to even distinguish the colour ... I would like to suggest they try the same but with RED. Maybe it's obvious, but what used to work for posters forever, probably still does ... they can break it into an orange type, strong red perhaps.

Best,

Hello,

Thanks for the new sketch.

I think these few milimeters already changed a lot. All in all you are right about the green. It is more beautiful than the red, more consistent. I will send the sketch to Francesca, I hope she likes the poster too. Then I have to fight with Peter and Paul ... as always. I will keep you informed.

Greetings,

Hello,

We looked once again at the poster, and also Francesca gave me her opinion. We both like the design, the typeface and so on, but we still think it is not very readable at first glance. We talked about this problem and came to the solution that we chose the wrong image. With such a dense image it is just not possible to transmit information in a very readable way - except if you set a white box at the top and on the bottom but that's something we don't want. So, once again, we and Francesca like the design of the poster, the typeface and so on, but we have to replace the image. Francesca made a suggestion (attached). Of course it is not worked out and there are still mistakes. The Museum name is missing the diacritics on the u, the image references. But this image would be good. You can download the high-resolution data from Francesca's web page. The username is 'photoeditor', the password 'passwordplease'.

Ok? Please call me if you have any questions.

Best,

Index

Is there such a thing as the most beautiful colour?
Does a colour have a meaning?
Are colours spiritual?
When is a colour meaningful?
Should I insist on the colour?
Is purple the most beautiful colour?
Will a beautiful typeface change the meaning of the word?
Is hand-writing more honest?

Can I discuss taste?
How do I avoid discussing taste?
Can taste be argued?
It looks good, but what is it?
What are good arguments?

Can it be done without having a discussion about it?
Would giving many options make it better in the end?
Are good discussions better than many options?
Should I work on something that might never happen?

Should I be more concrete?
How can I avoid misunderstandings?
How do I realise where the difficulty is?
Should I escape difficulties?
Should I drop it, or should I finish it?
Should I be stricter, harder and colder?
Should I be soft, warm and flexible?
How are decisions made?
Who should take control?

What makes a good relationship?
Should I work just with people I know?
Should I work just with people I can meet in person?
Should I have discussions in person?
Should I have discussions over the phone?
Should I have discussions in writing?

What should I commit to?
Should I commit to stapling 1500 books myself?
Should I commit to binding 1500 books myself?
Should I commit to preforating 1500 books myself?
Can I cut 10 posters into 16,000 pieces of confetti in two days?

When is graphic design a craft?
Should I know how it's made?

Should I say no, because it needs more time?
How many projects can I handle at the same time?
Is the nice thing about working that there's no time left?
Can I ask money for overtime?
How long does it take to make a book?
Do I need more than two days to design a poster?
Should I invoice the time I spend writing e-mails?

Can I make everybody happy?
Is it possible to make something beautiful for everybody?
Should I compromise?
What are the things I can't compromise on?
Should I always consider suggestions?
Is it important to be critical?
Am I too critical?
How does it work, when work is judged from different points of view?
What are opinions based on?

Do I know better when it's not my work?
Who's work is it?
Is it important that people can see I made it?

Should I always be involved in the content?
Is adding my own content necessary?
Should I go into editing as well?
Can I edit?
Should I just work with materials I can relate to?
Can I always relate?

Can I start with just the idea of what the content will be?
How much content do I need to have in order to start?

Am I just shaping the idea of what it is?
When do I know enough to know what it should be?
Can I shape it when it's not final?
Will the content ever be final?
Is it never final because it can always be changed?
Can I create context without content?

COLOPHON

Nowadays, if we speak about graphic design we can never be sure if we are actually talking about the same thing. The books in this series investigate different fields of graphic design where this lack of definition currently exists, as a means to contribute to the discussion and awareness of an arbitrary profession.

HARD SCHOOL BOOKS.
Graphic design department,
Gerrit Rietveld Academie,
Amsterdam, June 2007

CONCEPT & DESIGN
Dag Brandsaeter & Noa Segal
dbrandsater@gmail.com
noahaifa@gmail.com

EDITING
Dag Brandsaeter & Noa Segal

TRANSLATION
Hilde Meeus, Lukas Zimmer

PROOF-READING
Clare McNally

PUBLISHER
Veenman Publishers/Gijs Stork
Sevillaweg 140
3047 AL Rotterdam- NL
t. +31 10 245 3333
f. +31 10 245 3344

www.veenmanpublishers.com
ISBN 90-8690-103-6

DISTRIBUTION
D.A.P.
155, Sixth Avenue, 2nd floor
New York, NY 10013, USA
t. + 1 212 627 1999
dap@dapinc.com

Idea Books
Nieuwe Herengracht 11
1011 RK Amsterdam - NL
t. +31 20 622 6154
idea@ideabooks.nl

Art Data
12, Bell Industrial Estate
50 Cunnington Street
W4 5HB London- UK
t. +44 20 8747 1061
info@artdata.co.uk

info@veenmanpublishers.